HOW TO SAY "NO"

REGAIN CONTROL OF YOUR LIFE BY SETTING BOUNDARIES AND SAYING "NO" WITHOUT FEELING GUILTY

STEVEN HOPKINS

indirect, which are incurred as a result of the use of information contained within this document, including, but not limited to,
— errors, omissions, or inaccuracies.

CONTENTS

INTRODUCTION

It may sound like an odd thing in the current climate, where we're all being encouraged to be more positive and open to new ideas, possibilities, and adventures, but there are always instances where we need to say "no".

The thing is that so many of us are no good at saying "no". Not only are we not good at it, some of us are truly terrible at it, always giving in to requests from people who know exactly how to word things in order to get the better of us. Such people can be salespeople who are looking to make their sales quotas for the month, but they can also be people much closer to us.

It's not beyond the realms of possibility to believe

that a close and dear friend, or family member, might take advantage of your kindness. Yes, salespeople can be very good at spotting ways to manipulate people, hitting their weak spots, and we've always wanted to just turn a salesperson down without feeling guilty. But, for some of us, there is something that just doesn't allow us to disappoint other people. Unfortunately this is exactly what happens when we become accustomed to putting the needs of others before our own, and this is exactly the kind of behavior that this book is going to remove.

The disappointing thing is that often when we say "yes" to things we're forgetting what the real cost is to us, as individuals. Sure, in saying "yes" we're really helping another person out and lightening their load, but how about us? Who's helping us? ? Also, when I say "cost", I don't necessarily mean that in a financial sense. There is also a cost in terms of our time, our effort, and our mental well-being. These are all very important factors and we often do ourselves a grave disservice by dismissing these concerns, opting instead to please others.

Well, I'm here to tell you that you are no longer going to be that person who puts the well-being of others ahead of your own. You matter just as much as anybody else, and you are not going to let anybody treat you as if you're not. If you're reading this book you already know that you're the sort of person who finds it difficult, if not impossible, to say "no" to others, but you need to understand that you are not being honest with yourself, or with others, when you agree to doing something that you don't want to do.

It's not always easy to be honest with those we love, but it can often be just as hard to be honest with total strangers. It takes another level of maturity to be truly honest with the people around us, and that isn't always easy to say "no", especially when the people to whom we need to say "no" to are the ones who have become so used to hearing us say "yes" to their every demand.

If you want to have honest relationships with the people around you, you need to respect them enough to give them honest decisions. That is why it is so important to say "no" when you mean *no*, and that is why I'm here to walk you through this and make sure you learn to speak up and learn how to say "no".

I know how difficult it can be to say no, especially when we have been programmed all our lives to please others. We feel like saying yes makes us happy, and maybe it did in the beginning. But eventually we get to feeling like we're expected to say yes, and that doesn't feel so good anymore.

It's a burden, an expectation. Sometimes, we feel like it has become our identity, but we are more than that, and no matter how tough it may be to say "no", we need to find a way to not only say it, but to also be ok with having said it.

Yes, we want to be liked and we want to be kind, but we also need to be kind to ourselves. If you're reading this you are most likely someone who is not in the habit of being kind to yourself. That ends now, with this book. You have only one life, and it is your duty to live it to the fullest and live it for yourself. You can't go through life living to make the lives of others easier. Being judged, rejected, or disliked, is part and parcel of human life, no matter what you do, and no matter how often you say "yes" to things. If you want to say "yes", then by all means do so, but if you need to say "no", then you should do that and live your truth. Don't ever think of yourself as being less valuable than another, to the extent that you would stop being yourself.

You're going to read lots of my little stories along the way, through the course of this book, but let me give you a prime example of how I spent years doing the wrong thing, just because it pleased others. Before meeting my life coach, I spent years working a dead end office job. It gave me no pleasure, and it wasn't a challenge. I found it easy, but every time I tried to quit, my office manager would give me some story about how it wasn't a great time, asking me to stay another couple of months.

Without bragging, I was by far her best employee. Being the type who always wanted to please others, and not having another job lined up, I would always cave in and agree to stay a month or so. That would inevitably turn into another year. Eventually I met my life coach who got me to buck my ideas up. That's when I started working out, and got the confidence to leave my office job for real and set up my own business as a personal trainer.

Join me on this journey and we will have an in-depth discussion of how you can say "no" to people without you, or them, feeling bad about it. Follow my example, follow my steps and we'll soon have you taking back control of your life. Think of all the free time you'll have when you're no longer hamstrung by your inability to say "no" to requests. You'll have more time than you'll know what to do with, but that will be great because it will mean that the world is your oyster.

You'll finally have time to do all the things you've always wanted to do. Learn a new language, go traveling, start a business, start a family... I ended up doing all these things once I learned how to say "no". But it will only be a worthwhile experience for you if you follow my advice and learn not only from my examples, but also from my mistakes.

I'm only human and I've made a lot of mistakes, but I'm here to make sure you take the short-cut, bypassing all the wrong turns I made over time. So, let's work on this together so you get the most out of this book.

Chapter 1

WHY ARE WE AFRAID OF SAYING "NO"

> *I've always been afraid of saying no to people because I don't want them to be disappointed and dislike me.* - Elizabeth Gilbert

In this chapter we're going to be looking at some of the fundamental reasons why we struggle to say "no". Our inability to say "no" stems from a great many different sources and it can be difficult to land on why exactly we find it such a challenge. That is why we really need to take a good look at ourselves, and our behavior, and try to determine what the patterns are that lead us to need to please others.

Place your trust in me and let me walk you through some of the most common reasons why we have a problem with saying "no". As we go along be sure to see if any of these reasons may apply to you. Many people find this sort of thing daunting as they dislike examining their own behavior, but it is often highly beneficial and it's always good to be self-aware. Certainly it's something that I didn't like doing until I met my mentor, and life coach, who taught me the value of identifying patterns in my behavior. Remember that it is only when we find these patterns that we can make the necessary changes.

We struggle with low self-esteem

It is no surprise that some of us have low self-esteem.This is not some earth-shattering news, but it is something that we often take for granted, or assume that it doesn't apply to us. The truth is that we're understanding about others with low self-esteem, but often we just don't think that we fit into that category ourselves. Perhaps we feel that if we admitted that we had self-esteem issues we would be admitting to being some kind of *loser*. In fact, the opposite is true. It is only in facing up to reality, and admitting that we need help, that we can get what we need and begin taking the necessary steps.

But how does low self-esteem result in us saying "yes" to everything? Trust me when I tell you that it wasn't easy to face up to this one myself. As I already mentioned, my old boss used everything she could to get me to stay on, and it almost always worked. It was only when my life coach, Linda, helped me to see the underlying feelings and emotions that I realised that I actually felt as though I didn't deserve anything better. I said "yes" to people all the time, my self-esteem subconsciously making me believe that I did not deserve anything better.

We don't want to offend people

Many of the most common reasons why we have

trouble saying "no" are connected, so one reason may naturally lead to another. Our low self-esteem often means more than not believing that we deserve better. It often also manifests itself by making us do everything we can to avoid offending people. Of course, very few of us actually set out to offend others, but when you feel down about yourself that instinct to stay on the right side of everybody becomes so much more intense. It can lead us to think twice about what we actually want, suppressing our own needs in favor of the needs of people whom we want to like us.

What we need to understand is that saying "no" will not automatically mean that a person will be offended. If you're worried about offending people by saying "no", have you ever tried looking at it from a different point of view? Have you ever thought to yourself that if someone takes offense to hearing "no", then they have a problem they need to deal with, not you?

We want to avoid conflict

As I said before, many of the reasons that are

fundamental to our struggle with saying "no", are interlinked, and conflict is definitely something that we often see as being the result of causing offense. Rather than asserting our own will, we are often far more comfortable in meekly giving in to the wills of others. We would rather do something we don't want to, than risk a confrontation. We're afraid that saying "no" now may lead to an awkward situation later on, or that word will spread and we'll be ignored by a wider group of people.

Avoiding conflict does not necessarily need to mean avoiding the exchange of harsh words, or an altercation. It can also mean that we are keen to avoid causing someone else difficulty. You might say that you are happy to work an extra weekend shift, when actually you would rather be at home with your loved ones. The real reason you said "yes" was to avoid giving your manager a headache by having to find someone else to cover the shift, having to redo a rota.

We don't want to disappoint people

Like avoiding conflict, we also want to avoid disappointing people. The same circumstances apply, it's just that it involves different emotions. Rather than trying to avoid annoyance and anger from others, here you're trying to avoid disappointing people. In many ways the need to avoid letting people down can be more motivating than the need to avoid conflict. Some of us constantly yearn for and seek the approval of people whom we barely know, sacrificing the feelings of those to whom we are closest. However, others will naturally do everything they can to please their loved ones and avoid disappointing them.

The emotional urge to avoid seeing that look in their eyes can impose huge pressure on us. No one likes to see that crestfallen look in the eyes of their children, for example, but there is always a time when it is inevitable that we will not be able to give them the things they want, or spend as much time with them. For me, it was an old girlfriend whom I could never say "no" to. When I was getting my personal trainer business up and running I needed to spend as much time as possible on that, but I could never say "no" when she said she wanted to go out.

We want others to like us

This is one of the biggest factors that explains why we humans do many of the things that we do. Forget saying "yes", or "no", the need to be popular and liked is a huge motivating force for many of the things that we do in life. We want to be well regarded in the eyes of others, and this means a huge pressure to do the things that others want us to do, regardless of how it makes us feel.

Of course, there is nothing wrong in wanting to be liked. I'm not suggesting that it is a bad thing to want to be popular and liked, but it can often mean that we say "yes" when we really don't want to.

We have a people pleasing habit

Some of us just like to please others and get a thrill out of going the extra mile, even when we really don't have to. Essentially we get a kick out of seeing the look of pleasure, and even gratitude, that crosses their faces when we have gone above and beyond the call of duty. This comes from wanting to prove ourselves and show that we are worthy of their attention. We want them to think positively about us.

Even after I got married and had the respect of my wife's parents, I still found it difficult not to do everything I could to please them, often going to the extreme to be amenable and be liked by them. It was crazy because I already knew that I had their love, but I wanted more of it to feel secure about having their approval. Eventually it was my wife, Michelle, who had to tell me that my constant *trying* was making everyone feel uneasy.

What We've Learned

- There are many different reasons why we feel the need to say "yes" to everything that people ask of us. It is not always possible to narrow it down to one single reason.
- Low self-esteem can mean that we don't feel that we deserve to be able to say "no"

to others. Self-esteem issues can make us feel that it is our natural place in life to say "yes" to everything.

- Fear of offending people is another force motivating us to say "yes". We fear that someone will take offence to us asserting our own will, especially if they are used to hearing us say "yes" each time.

- Many of us choose to avoid conflict, preferring to avoid an exchange of words, an awkward situation that could lead to a frosty atmosphere. Also, we are often desperate to avoid imposing a difficult situation onto others, instead taking on the burden of an uncomfortable situation ourselves.

- The fear of disappointing people can weigh heavily on us, none of us like to see disappointment in the eyes of our loved ones, but some of us also have trouble causing people we don't know so well to be disappointed.

- Wanting to be liked, and to be popular, is not necessarily a bad thing. In fact it's something that most humans strive for. But it can be a bad thing when we take it to the extreme, saying "yes" to things we don't want to do.

- Some of us just need to please others and feel that warm glow that comes from having the approval of others, even if we already have it.

Chapter 2

COMING TO TERMS WITH
YOURSELF

66 *When I was around 18, I looked in the mirror and said, 'You're either going to love yourself or hate yourself.' And I decided to love myself. That changed a lot of things. -* Queen Latifah

You ou should now have a basic grasp of the different reasons why we feel the way we do when we deny ourselves the opportunity to say "no". Next, we're going to go through what you need to understand in order to change this behavior. It won't be easy as your "yes, boss" nature has become instinctive to you, part of your routine. I don't want to say that it is who you are, because you're about to change all that, but the change will not happen overnight. It will require some dedication so you shake off your *pleasing* habits.

1. Love Yourself

Are you scared of what people think of you? Do you lie awake at night wondering if people like what they see when they look at you? Do they value you as a person? Perhaps you are the type of person who chooses to concern yourself with such things, and I say *choose* because it is a choice. You can choose to turn off the voices that keep you up at night, or you can choose to continue listening to them and being too scared of what people will think when you say "no" to them. By refusing to say "no" you are only dragging yourself down.

Don't give in to all the negative things that try to tell you how much you're worth as a person. All you have to know is that you are worth far more than anyone will ever give you credit for. There is no point in estimating your worth, and self-esteem, against the appreciation that others show you. People hardly ever appreciate others as much as they should, this goes for those they are close to, as well as those they hardly know, perhaps even more so. The only way people are going to begin appreciating you like you deserve, is if you begin loving yourself. Learn to love yourself and you'll soon find that your self-esteem increasing like never before.

What's the best way to begin building your self-esteem? Simple. Start appreciating all the great things about yourself. If you find it difficult knowing where to start, think of all the people who are always asking things of you. All those people to whom you find it difficult to say "no". If it's just one person, think of all the times you've said "yes" to them for all those different requests. Know that the fact that they keep coming back to you means that you are important. If you're so important for all those tasks, you are definitely someone who should be taken seriously, and someone who should have more self-esteem.

2. Understanding when to say "no"

It's important to always remember that you have the right to say "no". You are your own person and you should be in control of your own life. It's always up to you whether you want to say "no" or "yes" to a request. Don't give others control over your life and don't allow others to speak for you. However, make sure that by saying "no" you won't be harming your work performance, or your school performance. It's important to pick and choose when to say "no", and also how to say it. Don't just say "no" because you don't feel like it, that would be cutting off your nose to spite your face.

I'm not saying that you should never say "no" to requests at work, but you need to weigh up their importance and relevance to what you are doing. If a request is totally in keeping with what you do in your daily work, then you probably need to comply if you want to keep your job. The same goes for your school work. It might sound like really basic advice, but it is still worth pointing out that it is important to know when and where to say "no".

However, if you are going to say "no" at work, or at school, then you should have a good excuse for it. Simply saying you "don't feel like it" isn't a good enough reason. Saying "no" because you don't have the time to fulfill whatever is being requested of you, that's easy to understand. We've all been there and we all know that things get hectic from time to time. It's better that you decline a commitment than take on too much and do a poor job of it.

The same goes for situations that make you feel uncomfortable. No one should expect you to say "yes" to doing something that would make you feel uncomfortable. If there is a situation at work, or at school, possibly with a colleague, that is awkward and makes you feel uncomfortable, you should feel perfectly within your rights to say "no" and decline the task. As covered already, it's also perfectly fine for you to say "thanks, but no thanks" to salespeople. Especially cold callers.

3. Don't worry

Worry is one of the key things that stops us from doing the things that we want to do, things that could very well lead to less worry. The problem is that we're too busy worrying about it to do the thing that could lead to less worry. Worry is the common denominator for all the reasons we covered in chapter 1 for why people have trouble saying "no" to others. The key to defeating this is to acknowledge that you have difficulty saying "no" because you have worries. Have a really good think about what stops you from saying "no" and I'm certain that you will be able to trace the roots of the issue back to some nagging worry at the back of your mind. What you have to do is admit that it is this worry that is holding you back.

Next thing you have to wrap your head around is that worrying about something is not likely to produce a positive outcome. Worry never solved anything, it only eats away at you, stressing you out and chipping away at your self-confidence, self-esteem and your peace of mind. Do you really think that this is the ideal basis for a good, healthy and balanced way to live your life? You know that it isn't, so it is time to tell yourself that worrying is a useless endeavor. But don't just tell yourself that, absorb that conclusion and really try to make it a part of your every day outlook.

We all spend far too much time worrying about what the potential outcome may be to various important decisions that we need to make. It's important to accept a decision when it has been made and not constantly rehash it, trying to find fault with the logic applied to the decision. In doing that you really are participating in an act of self-destruction, exactly the sort of thing that routinely tears down one's self-esteem. Worrying doesn't actually have an effect on anything. Worrying about a decision that you have already made will not change anything, it will only drag down your mental well-being.

Don't worry about saying "no", as long as it is in your own best interests. If you have said "no" to someone and you know that the logic behind that decision was taken with your best interests in mind, then you have nothing to worry about, and you have nothing about which to feel guilty. If your reasons for saying "no" were justified, then there is no one who should make you feel regret, or guilt for asserting your will, least of all yourself. So open a window in your mind and let all your worries fly out to disappear over the horizon. You don't need them and they are no longer welcome here.

4. Understand that "no" isn't rude

If you're the type of person who has always thought that saying "no" is rude, then you need to think again. Declining a person's request is not rude, or mean. It certainly does not mean that you will come across as uncaring. If that is what you're worried about, you should consider that the people closest to you will know you well enough by now to know that you are the furthest from a rude, uncaring person as it is possible to be.

If you're concerned about the impact that your "no" will have, you should understand that there are perfectly pleasant and socially acceptable ways to say it politely. You can say it without making any enemies, you can say it without feeling that sensation of regret skittering across your chest. You can have the self-confidence to turn someone down in a kind, but firm manner.

Poor impressions are not something that you need to worry about. People who know you know that you are a good person. Those who don't know you so well really have no business asking for your help with stuff. Other people don't worry that saying "no" will result in a poor impression, so why should you?

When I was a teenager I was something of a math whizz at my school, so I decided to use that skill to make a few extra bucks. I sold my services as a math tutor to families in my neighborhood, tutoring their kids in lower grades than me. Now when I look back on it I feel really stupid, but there was one family who declined my proposal to *tutor* their kid. However they did want me to *help* their kid. Difference being that I wouldn't get paid. Of course, fearing making a bad impression, I agreed. Their kid got free maths tutoring and I got... nothing. Sometimes, when we are too nice to others, it's ourselves that get hurt in the end.

What We've Learned

- Loving yourself is the first step towards gaining confidence and self-esteem.

- There is the right set of circumstances in which to say "no".
- Worry will not help you, or solve any problems.
- You can say "no" in a way that isn't rude and won't leave a bad impression.

Chapter 3

IMPORTANCE OF ASSERTIVENESS

" *I think naturally, if you're an actor, there's a high level of assertiveness that you need to have to survive this business. There's boldness in being assertive, and there's strength and confidence. - Bryan Cranston*

I n this chapter we're discussing a key element that will help you on your journey to discovering how to say "no". What is it? Assertiveness. Like I did all those years ago, you have trouble asserting yourself and sharing with others what is really on your mind. This behavior needs to stop and be replaced with a steel rod of determination and assertiveness that cannot be bent or snapped. Stick with me throughout this chapter and let's begin developing your assertiveness. There isn't a moment to lose!

Who are assertive people, anyway?

Assertive people get a bit of a bad rap. They are often thought of as arrogant troublemakers, but this isn't the truth about assertive people. Assertive people are people who are comfortable and confident in expressing their emotions, needs and opinions to others. This doesn't necessarily mean that they are forceful about how they do it. They are not necessarily imposing their views upon others, they're just not shy about expressing themselves. If you're having trouble saying "no" to people, you could do a lot worse than becoming a little more assertive.

If you've always thought of assertive people as acting in a certain way that would be alien to you, not in keeping with whom you are as a person, you should know that assertive people do not readily sacrifice their own needs and desires, just to please others. Isn't this just the sort of behavior you need to adopt? Assertive people are usually full of self-confidence and high self-esteem, exactly the sort of qualities that you need to adopt and develop in yourself if you are to tell people what you really want.

Being a good communicator is an essential part of telling people what you want and letting them know that you are not to be taken for granted. Get your feelings out of your chest and expose them for all to see. How? By being assertive and speaking up. Express yourself well to get your point across to others effectively. That is the only way that others will be able to recognize your feelings. After all, you can't blame people for not knowing how you feel when you don't tell them, can you?

Less anxiety and depression

Other than the ability to communicate your feelings and emotions to others and let them know that you do not agree to their requests, there are other benefits to becoming more assertive. Some of these benefits will be things that you had never even thought of. For example, did you know that a lack of assertiveness can lead you to feeling unful-filled and down?

When I was anticipating the birth of our first child, I was acutely aware that I needed to be earning more money. I had a young family to nourish and look after, so I reluctantly gave up the personal trainer business that I had developed and applied myself to other entrepreneurial pursuits. One of these was to develop products that I pitched to investors. There were some things in the mix that sound crazy to me now, and I think to myself that I can't believe that that was me doing those things. At the end of my pitches, I always used to feel a little down, regardless of whether it had been a success, or not. Why? Because I always felt that I could have been more confident, more forward about my product and why I thought it would be a success.

Not being able to put forward your point of view in an articulate and understandable way can lead us to feeling inadequate. After those pitches, I always felt bad about not being good enough at pitching, but actually it was my assertiveness that could have used a shot in the arm. When we feel that we have given in to the requests of others, without making ourselves properly understood, we can begin to feel down about ourselves, disappointed at our relative inability to stand up for ourselves. In a way, we feel that our rights have been violated by another person and that they have taken advantage of our good nature in order to get what they wanted from us. Nobody wants to be taken advantage of and if it goes on for too long, these feelings of inadequacy will only accumulate. It is best to nip them in the bud by developing your assertiveness.

Improves self-confidence and self-esteem

Assertiveness is made up of two vital things: self-confidence, and self-esteem. It is important to have both of these things. People often think that they are one and the same, but that isn't true.

Self-esteem is the confidence you have in your own worth, or abilities; whereas self-confidence is the pure conviction that you have in yourself, your abilities and your judgement. Use your self-confidence to liberate yourself from uncertainty and you will not only find yourself taking action more readily, but also, with the positive thinking behind your actions, they are more likely to succeed.

Whether we realize it or not, self-confidence plays a significant role in our lives. Those without self-confidence not only have difficulty in getting things done, but they don't know what they want to get done in the first place. They are usually the people who have no ambitions, no aims, and no goals.

Self-esteem, self-confidence, and assertiveness. These are the keys to improving your life and getting what you want from it.

Stop a time bomb

Lack of assertiveness often leads to frustration because you realize that there is a problem, you just don't know what the problem is. In situations like this, many of us tend to lash out at others, usually the people who are closest to us. In not asserting yourself, you are handing over control of your life to others – people who have very little interest in your comfort; people who fully expect you to comply because that's all you've ever been to them: a compliant, pliable person.

Don't let this frustration boil over into aggression. It is very common for those who are not particularly assertive to let the frustrations mount and build until it explodes into aggressive behavior that others will find shocking and distasteful.

Makes you more likable

Did it ever occur to you that people like assertiveness? They find it comforting and reassuring as they know where they stand with people who readily express themselves and let others know how they are feeling. As I said before, it's not surprising that people continue to make requests of you when you don't tell them how you feel about it.

Assertive people have better relationships with everyone around them as they know what they want, what they need, and they know how to ask for it. People like this in their relationships as it fosters a greater sense of harmony and makes for a more satisfying interpersonal experience.

Be better at goal setting

Develop your assertiveness and you'll soon find yourself making plans and drawing up lists. Plans? Lists? Yes, because you'll have so much motivation to discover the things you want to do with your time and your life. With the confidence and self-esteem, you'll have so many new ideas for what you want to do and how to achieve your new goals. You'll soon be sharing your new aims and ambitions with your friends and colleagues. Pretty soon you'll be the one asking them to help you out with meeting your goals. And after all this time of asking you for favors, they had better help out!

Be able to communicate confidently

If you're one of those people who constantly worries about how you will be perceived if you say "no" to a request, you'll find that some extra assertiveness will go a long way to resolving this. With some extra assertiveness you'll have the confidence to successfully navigate situations that you fear will be uncomfortable or delicate. For the first time in your life, you will not live in fear of saying "no". You'll be taking back control of your life using a clear and assertive communication style that will earn you the respect of your peers. You really will be building the path to a new life and career full of potential and opportunities for happiness.

Make great managers

Assertive people make great managers because they have goals and aims in mind and they are not afraid to deploy people as needed to get things done. Assertive people are not afraid to approach people and ask things of them because they treat people with fairness and respect. In turn they are the same, forming the cycle of fairness and respect needed for projects to succeed. Yet another reason why assertive people are often well-liked and trusted as leaders who have the support of those working under them.

What We've Learned

- It is a good thing to be assertive. Being assertive does not necessarily mean being forceful or rude.

- In not being assertive you are risking becoming frustrated and depressed at your inability to make yourself, your feelings understood.
- Assertiveness is made up of self-esteem and self-confidence. Use both of these to fight your inability to say "no".
- Those who cannot express themselves often find that those pent-up emotions, and feelings of frustration, build and build to potentially an aggressive outburst.
- People tend to get on better with those who are assertive as it is easier to know where one stands with an assertive person.
- Assertive people know what they want and are therefore better at setting goals for themselves.
- Being better communicators, assertive people are unafraid to tackle potentially awkward situations.
- Assertive people have the knack for managing people in a way that is productive and universally satisfying.

Chapter 4

HOW TO BECOME MORE ASSERTIVE

> *Women who are assertive and have confidence, qualities older women possess. They've been on the Earth a little longer. They're more seasoned. They don't play games. They know what they want, and they're not afraid to tell you.* - Taye Diggs

Of course, it's all very well telling people that they need to be more assertive, but how does one actually go about that? After all, assertiveness isn't something that we're all naturally born with. Even those who have been assertive all their lives can have something happen to them that takes that confidence away. We're all vulnerable to the things that happen to us in the natural course of life.

Perhaps you cannot remember ever being assertive, or perhaps you were once assertive, but something occurred to take away your assertiveness. How do we go about developing those assertive qualities for the first time? What do we need to do to recapture those qualities of self-confidence and high self-esteem that we used to have? In this chapter we will be answering those questions, and more.

Value yourself, your time and your interests

The first step on your journey to becoming more assertive is to take a good look at yourself, your thoughts, the patterns in your behavior. It is only in doing this that you will achieve a good enough understanding of yourself, and your behaviour. This is essential if you are going to begin making changes to the way you think and behave. This will in turn have an effect on the way your confidence, and eventually your ability to say "no".

In understanding how you currently operate, you will develop a better and deeper appreciation of your inherent value, as well as the value you offer to those around you. It doesn't matter whether it's your colleagues at work, or your close family members at home, you offer certain qualities to each and you need to believe strongly in all that you bring to those different tables.

Remember that your self-belief will be the basis of your self-confidence, providing the foundation for your burgeoning assertive behavior. Self-belief is crucial if you're going to become more assertive, but in order to have self-belief you also need to develop the capacity to believe in yourself. This means admitting that have a range of good qualities and choosing to believe in that.

A good level of self-belief will go a long way to helping you recognize and accept that you deserve to be treated with dignity and respect. Self-belief and assertiveness will push you to defend your rights, stick up for yourself and no longer will you sacrifice your own needs and desires to satisfy those of others.

You need to understand that your self-worth

should not be any less than anybody else's. You are a valuable human being who has a lot to contribute to the world. Those who understand this about themselves, and believe in it, feel happier and more in control of their lives.

Use of body language

Your mouth isn't the only way that you can communicate your needs and feelings. Of course, you can also use your body language to communicate these things. That's why you need to learn to pay attention to how you use your body when communicating with others. Even when you're not consciously communicating with others, your body is still saying things, giving things away, that you aren't aware of.

Take eye contact, for example. Eye contact is something that we learn to use from a very young age and we all have an understanding of what different looks can signify. With eye contact the quality of your communication with another person is impacted by the level of eye contact you maintain with them as you're talking.

Eye contact is a simple example, but how about posture? The way you carry yourself says a lot about your confidence levels and how you feel. A slouching position signifies boredom or indifference, whereas a rigid position can connote that you are not comfortable at all, tense and ill at ease. Even if you are not entirely comfortable, it can help you to exude a feeling of self-confidence and assertiveness if you can look comfortable. So, try to find a comfortable standing position that works for you. The same goes for sitting, you don't want to slouch and create the wrong impression.

Your body movement is a big part of your identity and each of us has our own particular ways of moving that are unique to us. Be mindful about how you use your body in order to say the right things about yourself and express yourself the way you want to. Your body language is your ally and it is necessary if you want to affirm your point with conviction.

Listen actively

Good communication is as much about what you

don't do as it is about what you do. What does that mean? Be sure not to interrupt anyone else when they are trying to express their point of view. Nobody likes to be interrupted and the chances are good that you will agree with this as you yourself have been interrupted in the past. If you wish people to accord you the same courtesy, then it is advisable that you rein in the temptation to add your views to something someone is in the middle of explaining.

Listening skills are not just something you put down on your resume to pad it out. They are real things and it is always worth taking a little time to refresh your knowledge of them. If you want people to listen attentively to what you have to say, you need to make sure you listen carefully to what they have to say. This doesn't just mean passively listening and making the right noises at the right times, it means actually listening so you can ask questions when they're done, or make your own comments, adding your own point of view.

Listening actively really is a skill that everyone should master as we could all do with being better at listening, hearing and understanding what others have to say. Yes, listening to others is a key part of being assertive. Remember that this is one of the key differences between being assertive and arrogant.

Be Open to Criticism and Compliments

Again, a difference between being assertive and arrogant is in being open to compliments, but also being open to criticism. Those who are arrogant do not know how to listen to the views of others, making them especially bad at taking criticism. Those of us who are assertive are not only good at taking in the views of others, understanding their standpoints, appreciating the intentions behind their words, they also possess the capacity to take on board those comments and turn them into something positive by making changes where appropriate to make themselves better.

Of course, when you're starting out on this journey, it can be difficult to take compliments, let alone criticism. If you're coming from a place where you have very little self-belief and self-confidence, you'll not only receive criticism, but you'll see it in places where it doesn't actually exist. Moreover, you'll be ready to believe all the criticism you encounter. Does that sound familiar? That was definitely the case for me when it came to being a father for the first time. I bent over backwards trying to please everybody, but all it took was a little grumble from my wife about something trivial to make me feel like I was failing at everything. Even when she complimented me on something I would somehow turn it around to make it into a criticism, concentrating on the overcooked chicken in the pasta dish I'd made for dinner, rather than the great flavors.

Remember that even when you do encounter criticism you need to keep an open mind about it. Not every piece of criticism you receive will be well-deserved. If you feel that this is the case, you need to be prepared to challenge your critic, but do so in a constructive, level headed way. You don't need to become defensive or angry to argue your point. By all means, engage someone who has a criticism, but be aware that they may not see things from your point of view, it's a case of explaining yourself.

In all cases, whether it's criticism or compliments, accept the feedback graciously, humbly and positively. It is only by acting in this way that you can take a position of power and control. If you get upset at criticism you are giving your critics control. If you choose not to believe compliments, thinking that people are simply being kind and overlooking your shortcomings, you are simply missing out on a potential boost to your self-belief.

When it comes to feedback, positive or negative, you need to look past your emotional reactions and take the opportunity to effect significant, positive change. If it's criticism, consider what you can do to change. If it's a compliment, change what you're doing by doing more of it!

Learn to Say "No"

Developing your assertiveness should help a lot with developing your ability to say "no". You don't need me to tell you that it is hard to say "no"; that is why you're reading this book. In the beginning, at least, it will continue to be difficult for you to say "no", but a simple trick is to just not say "yes". Often, especially when you're put on the spot, people will want you to say "yes", but remember that you don't have to.

Know your limits and your optimal workload. There is no point in taking on more work than you can handle and do well. Having a keen appreciation of how much work you can comfortably handle will help you to manage your tasks more effectively. Be strict about this limit, don't persuade yourself to sneak an extra half hour here or there to fit something else in. In whittling down your workload to a comfortable level you should be able to pinpoint where others may be taking advantage of your good nature.

The most important thing to you should be your time and your workload, so don't be afraid to say "no", despite how difficult it is.

What We've Learned

- Learn to value yourself. You are no less valuable than anyone else.
- Your body says almost as much as your mouth, so pay attention to what it's saying.
- Listen carefully to others when they are sharing their views, if you want them to reciprocate.
- Learn to take criticism, but also accept

compliments, with grace, humility and an open mind.

- Say "no" when you need to. Plan your optimal workload to better identify how and where others may be taking advantage of you.

Chapter 5

HOW TO SAY NO WITHOUT HURTING ANYONE'S FEELINGS

" *You have a right to say no. Most of us have very weak and flaccid 'no' muscles. We feel guilty for saying no. We get ostracized and challenged for saying no, so we forget it's our choice. Your 'no' muscle has to be built up to get to a place where you can say, 'I don't care if that's what you want. I don't want that. No.'* - Iyanla Vanzant

I get it. You've always wanted to be the kind of person who can say "no" to people. You just don't want to offend them, or come off as rude or arrogant. Firstly, you should know that saying "no" does not make you rude, or arrogant. You have every right to let people know how you really feel. You just need to find the right way to go about it. You're a mature person, so you know that for everything in life there is a right way and a wrong way to do it. As long as you decline their request in the right way, there is no reason why you should feel bad. This is what we'll be covering in this chapter, so strap in as we take a look at the building blocks that form the foundations of saying "no" without hurting anyone's feelings.

Be honest and straightforward

Of course the simplest way to get yourself out of a situation where someone is asking you to do something for them is to politely say: "no", and then give them an appropriate reason. No one is suggesting that you just say "no". Always be kind and courteous when declining an invitation to do something for someone else, but also be firm. Giving a good reason is part of being firm. A good reason is the perfect back up to you saying "no" to someone.

If you're the sort of person who is always concerned and worried about how you are going to look to others if you say "no", you need to understand that saying "no" does not automatically give you a negative image. On the contrary, as mentioned before, you should actually gain credibility as someone who only agrees to things when they have sufficient time to do a good job. You could even use this as part of your good excuse. "No, sorry, I can't. I simply don't have the time at the moment to do a good enough job of it. I wouldn't want to do it wrong." Nobody will want you to do a sub-par job and they should be happy that you have been honest and open with them. Being honest like this will only add to your good reputation.

If it's something of a more personal nature it is always a good policy to give a little more of an explanation, especially if you don't want the same request to crop up every so often. Let's take a trite storyline beloved of sitcoms everywhere. A friend asks you out on a date, but you're not sure that you want to start a romantic relationship with them, preferring to maintain the friendship that you both enjoy. Do you do the typical sitcom thing of making up excuse after excuse every other day? Or, do you be honest and transparent, telling them:

"I'm flattered that you've asked me, but I haven't thought of you in that way because I enjoy our friendship so much. I wouldn't want anything to ruin that. I hope you understand, and I hope that this won't make things awkward between us."

Avoid inventing excuses or lying

Again, we've all seen sitcom episodes where one lie leads to another, and another. Life is far too short and you're far too good a person to be doing that sort of thing. Lies and fabrications will only bring you down and make you feel bad. So don't do it. Be yourself, open and transparent and you will find that people will respond well to that. Lies will only work in the short-term, but they are always found out and that's when you'll regret being dishonest. If you want to avoid hurting anyone's feelings, you need to avoid lying, as few things are more hurtful than realizing that someone you trusted has been lying to you.

Make a counter offer

This is something that few people actually try doing, especially those who are lacking in self-confidence. But it is very effective in getting another person to be flexible about what they want. Making a counter offer is a strategy that you should use when you're in a situation where you really don't want to say no, but you have to. It could be that you don't have enough time to fulfill their request, it could be that you have promised yourself a little space for relaxation, or it could be that you're going away for the weekend.

Negotiating a compromise with someone is great when you don't necessarily want to say "no", but instead you want to help on your own terms. Often when people come with requests they'll present it in a way that's best for them, such as: "Can you help me to finish this, I need it by the end of the week?" Usually it will be fine for them to have it by the beginning of Monday and there is no harm in suggesting this to them. If you have a good reputation for helping people, and if you're reading this then you definitely do, they will be more than happy to place their faith in you.

Remember that things are rarely set in stone, so when someone comes to you with a request that they need fulfilled by certain time, there is usually some wiggle room. If it's something that you genuinely do want to help out with, ask for some flexibility. You may not have the time immediately, but, "in a few days I'll have more time on my hands. Will that work for you?" You're not saying "no", but instead you're offering a compromise, a counter offer, a perfectly socially acceptable and mature way for people to work together. Helping someone doesn't need to be entirely on their terms. If they're the ones who need your help, they should be willing to accommodate you, don't you think?

Suggest a retry later

Another way to not say "no" when you genuinely want to help, but can't do so immediately, is to suggest that they try you again later. Why not? That's not rude, it's not likely to hurt anyone's feelings, it's perfectly reasonable and you should be doing it a lot more. Later on in my career when I was working in digital marketing I was bombarded with requests for help from my young employees who were still gaining experience in the field, little did they know that I didn't know much more than them. Of course, being the *boss*, I wasn't in a position to just say "no". It was always a case of "come back to me again in half an hour and I'll help you out with that". I wasn't paying them lip service, I meant it. Sure, sometimes they'd come back to me and I'd still be busy, but I always kept my word and eventually helped them out.

If you're going to do a "try me again, later" you need to be firm about it and let them know that there is no point in badgering you to have help now. Later means *later*. If it's a salesperson, for example, and the thing that they're selling really is something that you might be interested in at another time, it is best to be honest and straight with them. "It's winter, so no, I really don't need my windows cleaned right now, but check back with me in spring." Or: "I'm impressed with your presentation but no, I don't need a loft conversion right now. Tell you what, leave me your card and I'll get back to you when things change."

Use humility

Humility is a great way to get out of a sticky situation. Imagine that someone at work wants you to take on a little more responsibility, not that difficult to imagine, right? Well, you can always suggest that, as flattered as you are by their attention, you aren't their best choice for the job. "Thanks for thinking of me, but I don't have that much experience with that, so I'm not sure that I'm the best choice."

As discussed earlier, people will respect the fact that you want to do the best job that you can, and would rather forgo the opportunity than offer substandard results. They'll see you as someone who always wants to offer the high quality and the best results.

What We've Learned

- The simplest thing to do is to just say "no", preferably backed up by a good excuse.
- Being straight with people and saying "no" will only enhance your reputation, so you have no reason to believe that people will have negative thoughts about you.
- At times saying "no" will undoubtedly need to be backed up with a bit more of an explanation.
- Try to make a counter offer in situations

where you really don't want to say "no".
Make sure you don't do this for every
situation where you don't want to
disappoint someone, or you'll soon find
that you're making counter offers for
everything, instead of saying "no".

- Negotiating a compromise is a mature way
  for people to come to an agreement, and
  the counter offer is a great way to offer
  help on your own terms.

- If someone needs your help, it shouldn't
  be entirely on their terms, they should be
  able to give you some wiggle room if they
  really want your assistance.

- Don't be afraid to ask someone to try you
  again later, but be firm about when you
  will be available to help.

- If it's a salesperson, be firm that it is a
  "no", but be polite and offer to reconsider
  their offer in due course.

- Humility is a great tool, so use it. Be
  honest about not having the best
  experience for a task and you'll be
  respected for wanting to do the best.

Chapter 6

HOW TO SAY NO WITHOUT FEELING GUILTY

> *People tend to dwell more on negative things than on good things. So the mind then becomes obsessed with negative things, with judgments, guilt and anxiety produced by thoughts about the future and so on.* - Eckhart Tolle

I f you have been living for some time with the belief that saying "no" to someone is something for which you should feel guilty, it will be difficult to persuade yourself otherwise. But you must try, all the same, because saying "no" is not always an option, it is sometimes necessary and you need to be able to do it without feeling guilty afterwards. As I have said before, there is no reason for you to feel guilty for looking out for yourself. You are valuable, and your feelings matter just as much as the needs of others, so don't imagine for a moment that they do not.

Be true to yourself

Don't forget that when you are being true to yourself, you are also putting yourself in a position to be honest with others about how you feel. It is important to value your own thoughts, feelings and emotions. Without such honesty you won't be able to get what you really need by saying "no" to requests. Be honest with yourself about what you need and then you can figure out what the best way is to get that. Remember: "If you're on good terms with yourself, you're on good terms with others."

Being true to yourself, and others, is all about communication. If you can communicate with yourself and understand what is best for you, you can communicate with others and let them know what you need. As I said earlier in this book, you can't blame others for not knowing what you need when you haven't communicated that to them. Let out your truth, but don't just keep it to yourself. Let it out into the world so everyone knows what you need. People can be a lot more giving than you think. Letting them know what you need will often result in getting just that.

We don't always feel like being helpful, even if we do have the time, and it's okay to feel like this. We're all human and we're allowed to have our idiosyncrasies and our different moods. We don't feel the same way all the time and there is no shame in being honest and admitting that to yourself. On the contrary, in being honest with yourself about this you should feel like a weight has been lifted from your shoulders. If you don't feel like helping someone out, just don't. Helping someone when you can, and when you want to, is good, but sacrificing your time and energy when you don't want to will not be good for you, or the person you're helping.

As mentioned before, you don't have to be rude about it, but it is essential that you are open and honest with others about your feelings. So, don't be afraid to express yourself and let everyone know how you feel, even if it means that someone ends up being disappointed. Sometimes you just need to do what is best for you, even if that lets people down, but don't feel bad about it, you're allowed to have your own time, space and feelings.

Be true to your principles

What are your principles? What are your convictions? These are not always easy questions to answer, but you need to remain true to those principles and convictions if you're going to learn to say "no" to people who constantly make requests of your time and efforts. When we feel a little vague on what we really need, that is when we begin to feel guilty about saying "no" to people. We feel that while we have all that is necessary to help them, we are blowing them off in order to... we're not sure. Determine what is important to you and stick to your guns.

Don't let others sway you and persuade them to help you if you don't want to. Peer pressure is a real thing, and it's not only for teenagers. Adults are also susceptible to pressure from others and giving in to such manipulation will only leave you feeling disappointed that you were not able to assert yourself more forcefully from the outset. That's right, you'll wish you had paid more attention to Chapter 3! It is far better to make a single firm stand for yourself, and your principles, by saying "no", rather than spending months fulfilling the requests of others and feeling terrible about it.

Many people avoid saying "no" because they're afraid of creating awkward situations for themselves at work, or within their social circle. They are afraid of making enemies, they would rather remain on good terms with everyone by giving in to their demands, than make an enemy. Guess what? If you think you have made an enemy by saying "no" to them, then they weren't your friend in the first place. At least you'll know that you stood up for the right thing, something that is important to you. There is no shame in that as long as it is true to you.

Be true to your priorities

We all have certain things that are important to us. For some it is our jobs, our careers, doing everything that we can in order to get ahead and make the best situation for ourselves. For others it is family that is the most important thing. We do everything we can now in order to make life better for our children and spend more time with them later on in life. What are your priorities? Perhaps there are other things that are more important to you, not careers, or family, but other things. That's fine, but whatever it is, figure it out and establish it as your priority.

If you find it difficult to ascertain your principles, and convictions, work on your priorities. Collecting a list of priorities, and ordering them, should at least be a little easier and offer you a good base from which to make decisions about what you will say "yes" to and how often you will accept a request to help people. Again, I know I've said this before, but it is very important, remember that there is no shame in saying "no". On the contrary, the fact that you do say "no" to things means that you are staying true to your priorities and convictions.

Trust me on this, once you have set yourself a list of priorities, and remember that it doesn't need to be a long list, it can be just one or two things, saying "no" to people becomes much easier. Why? Because it becomes much clearer to see what is really important to us and focus on that. Use your list of priorities as the blueprint by which you make your decisions about whether to say "yes" or "no" to someone. Once you begin doing this it will become more than accepting, or declining, a request for help, it will be about making the right decision.

Change your orientation

Many people just feel that they have no other option but to feel guilty when they say "no". They believe that saying "no" is inherently wrong, subconsciously believing that other people are more worthy than they are. They believe that the desires of others are pressing than their own, so they sacrifice their own wants, needs, principles, priorities in order to satisfy the needs of those who request their help.

Perhaps you're one of these people who feels that it is wrong to put your own needs ahead of the desires of others. If that is indeed you, it is time for a little reprogramming. Don't worry, I'm not going to hypnotize you. Instead you are going to help yourself by making the time to really think about that feeling of guilt when it comes over you. Don't push it away, don't ignore it. Instead, really consider that feeling of guilt and what it means, its ramifications.

I'm not asking you to feel guilty about feeling guilty. Instead, I'm asking you to think about that guilt and ponder where it comes from and why you really feel it. What is it that makes you feel that it is bad to say "no". Perhaps it is a feeling from a lesson learned in the past, but that no longer applies.

What We've Learned

- Learn to be honest with yourself about what you need. It is only in knowing what you need that you will be able to communicate with yourself and others in a way that will get you those things.
- No one should expect you to always be in the mood to help. Sometimes you just don't feel like it, and that's ok.

- If you need to let people down, that's okay, as long as you are honest with yourself about what you need.
- Determine your principles and convictions. Figure out what is important to you, and then stand by it!
- Don't give in to peer pressure. Don't do things just to remain popular. Stick to your guns!
- If you feel that you have made an enemy of someone by saying "no" to them, then they weren't your friend in the first place. You should feel proud of sticking up for what you believe in.
- If establishing principles and convictions was a tough ask, try making a list of convictions.
- Setting priorities will help you to establish what types of requests for help you will accept, and also how often you can afford to do that.
- Your list of priorities will become the blueprint by which you accept or decline to help others. It will become your guide to making the decision that is right for you.

- If you feel that you should not put your needs ahead of the desires of others, you need to take a good look at the guilt that you feel when you do that. Why do you feel that guilt? Where does it come from?

Chapter 7

BONUS CHAPTER: USEFUL WAYS TO SAY NO IN DIFFERENT SITUATIONS

Having me discussing how it is imperative that you say "no" more often is all well and good, but what I've learned from personal experience is that people learn more readily when they are presented with a visual example.

Unfortunately I can't include videos with this book, but what I can do is illustrate some examples of requests and how you can respond to them using the techniques that we have gone through. You can picture the scene for yourself.

It is my sincere hope that you will find the

following examples not only helpful but practical. I've selected examples that I think are the kind of situations that most people reading this book will face most often.

How to say "no" to a friend asking you for a favor

Friends are one of the worst perpetrators when it comes to asking for help. Remember when I discussed priorities? If you're reading this book then things have gotten serious and you need to determine whether you still want this person as a friend, or not.

If yours is a true friendship, but they tend to ask for a lot of favors, they should get the message when you tell them: "No thanks, I would, but I just don't have the time right now. You remember what I was telling you the other day, right?" If they're a real friend they'll remember what you were talking about and understand. If they're faking it they'll be reluctant to reveal they hadn't been listening.

How to say "no" to friends asking you out

Okay, for this one the favor they're asking may be as much to do with you getting out, as it is with them having a buddy to accompany them. There could be a thousand reasons why you don't feel like going out, but maybe your friend feels that they are doing you a favor by getting you out of the house.

For this one I would suggest using the "try me again, later" approach. Tell them you are enthused at the prospect of going out, but that you'll have to leave it for another time. If it's getting to the end of the month, maybe things are a little tight and it's a choice between paying bills and going out. Just be honest, they'll understand. "I'd really like to, but I'm waiting to get paid. How about next weekend?"

How to say "no" to family get-togethers

Family get-togethers can be the greatest, but they can also be the worst, especially when you feel like the odd one out in the group. We've all been there and said something to our parents like: "I just have a lot going on right now," which just made them worry even more and insist that they come around to visit. Instead, try: "I'm really excited to see you and hang out, but I want it to be an occasion when I can really have some quality time with you all."

How to say "no" to family visits

If the previous answer didn't work and you've found yourself facing a situation where your family have invited themselves over to your place, you need to be firm. "No, I need to spend some time alone so I can sort through my life and decide what I want to do next. But I'm always keen for your advice, so let me call you." Family always like to feel needed and they love being asked for advice, so it's a good way to make a successful counter offer. Also they always like to hear that you're getting your life in order.

How to say "no" to your neighbor who ask you to babysit their pet

We all have that one neighbor who always catches us at a vulnerable moment to ask a favor. "Can you do this for me?" "Can you do that for me?" It's always one thing or another. The most effective way to handle them asking for you to pet-sit is to point out that you are not the best candidate for this particular honor. They will only want the best person to look after their pride and joy. Try: "Well, I'm happy to do it, of course, but I'm not a pet owner myself, so I'm not really the best person for it, am I? Surely the ideal person would be someone with a pet?"

How to say "no" to requests from strangers

Unless if you're one of those people who finds it imperative to make a good impression on strangers, you should find them the easiest people to whom to say "no". Imagine someone is asking you for *cuts* in a queue. You can easily, and honestly, say: "No, if I gave you cuts, I'd have to give cuts to everyone and then where would I be?" Or, you can try: "I only give cuts to people I know, so no."

How to say "no" to salespeople

When it comes to salespeople it is always tempting to simply hang up the phone. Maybe you've done this before and felt a rush of guilt afterwards. Well, it's always best to not be rude, but we all have lapses now and then. Imagine that this is a salesperson that you have invited into your home to give you an estimate for renovating your kitchen. They have given you the price and are pressuring you for an answer. Be honest: "Thanks for the estimate, but no, I'm not deciding now, I'd like to sleep on it."

How to say "no" to telephone sellers

I've already covered hanging up the phone in the last example, always a possibility, but not recommended as it is quite rude. Let's imagine that this is a person who has called you and made a pitch for their product. Instead of hanging up you can try: "You've given me a lot to think about. I'm going to think about it and get back to you if I decide to go ahead."

How to say "no" to someone who asks to borrow money

It should be easy enough to say "no" to a stranger asking to borrow money: "No, I don't lend money to strangers." I mean, who does, right? However, when it comes to people that you do know, friends and family, it isn't so easy. Or is it? Next time someone asks, tell them: "I'm going to say no, because money between friends and family always leads to trouble, I wouldn't want anything to come between us."

How to say "no" to a person you're not romantically interested in

This can be a bit of a minefield, especially if it's someone at work, or someone you know quite well and with whom you have mutual friends. If it's someone at work you can say: "I don't think it's a good idea to date people I work with." For a friend, try: "That would be really nice, but honestly, you're a friend whom I really value, so I wouldn't want anything to come between us."

How to say "no" to your boss

Your boss can be a little more of an intimidating prospect than others because you always want your boss to look favorably upon you. But saying no to them does not need to be difficult. Imagine they are asking you to work a weekend shift: "I'm sorry, but no, thank you. I promised my kid I'd have some quality time with them this weekend." No one can argue with parent/child time.

How to say no to your client

Perhaps your work involves dealing with clients who like to be cheeky and see if they can get away with adding things to a contract at the last minute. Stand firm and tell them: "No, I'm sorry but we would need more time to negotiate that before adding it to the contract. It may result in a higher fee."

How to say no to your other half

When it comes to family, things always get a little more difficult. We expect them to cut us some slack, which they usually do, but the trouble is that we don't cut ourselves any. Instead we bend over backwards to please them. Next time your other half asks you to pick up the kids from school instead, try countering with: "Well, can you pick them up the next time it's my turn?"

How to say no to your children

Perhaps the hardest thing in the world is to say "no" to our children. Maybe it's because we always want to give them everything that they want. Maybe it's because each time we look at them we see the vulnerable baby that they were when we first met them. In any case, it's natural, and healthy, to need to tell them "no" from time to time. Next time they want junk food instead of something healthy, tell them: "No, this is healthier and more affordable. You can have the junk food, if you'd like, but you'll have to go without something else."

How to say no to your parents

Saying "no" to our parents can be one of the most heartbreaking things, especially as they get older and we feel that we need to take care of them, just like they did us for so long. But you do need to stick to your priorities and, if you have your own family, they are now your priority. "No, I'm not going to be able to do that because I've promised to spend more time with the kids." I'm sure that your parents will understand.

CONCLUSION

If you have made it this far I thank you from the bottom of my heart. You have been a loyal reader and I hope that you have found this to be a fascinating read that has touched on more than a few home truths. My aim was to leave you with a lot to think about. If you are intent on following up this book with a thorough session of introspection, then I will have achieved my aim.

Over my years as an entrepreneur setting up businesses, in America, but also in other parts of the world, it has become apparent that we are becoming less accustomed to reading, listening, absorbing the insights that others have to share. So, in reading this book, you have definitely proved yourself to be one of a shrinking section of the world that is still open to alternative views.

By admitting to yourself that you need some help to change for the better, you are already empowered and should feel proud of yourself for taking the initiative to better yourself. I hope that this book has provided you with some of the insights that you were seeking, and I hope that it has broadened your horizons, at least just a little.

In Chapter One, we went through some of the biggest reasons why people feel compelled to say "yes" to everything. Low self-esteem, fear of offending others, the need to avoid conflict, fear of disappointing others, the need to be liked, the need to please... these are all crucial factors that we need to combat if we're serious about making progress fighting the urge to accept any and all requests from people for our help.

The key to fighting all those factors is boosting our own assertiveness, but before you can do that you need to get a few other things under your belt. This is a process with no long-term quick fixes. If you want a long-term solution you need to do the work, and in this case the work will involve learning to love yourself. This will help you to gain confidence and boost your self-esteem. Remember that worrying will not help you. Worry will not change the result of something, it can only bring you down and make you feel bad, affecting your self-esteem.

Absorb the fact that saying "no" does not automatically constitute a rude response, and you should not feel bad about it. The same goes for assertiveness, it's not a bad thing to be assertive, and it does not mean being rude, or aggressive. On the contrary, those who are assertive tend to be better communicators as they let people know what they want and need, making them easier to get along with. By stifling your assertiveness you are actually risking pent-up frustration and potentially an aggressive outburst.

Becoming more assertive will mean learning that your feelings, time and energy are no less valuable than anybody else's. It will also mean learning a little about your body language, as well as using your listening skills and showing attention if you wish to receive it in return. Remember that being assertive is as much about reacting as it is about acting. You don't always need to be driving things to be assertive, you can sit back and take criticism and praise from others, but learn to take them both well.

Your assertiveness will help with saying "no" with conviction, but in a sensitive way that doesn't hurt others. You can communicate your feelings to others in ways that are sensitive to particular circumstances. If you find yourself faltering, make a list of priorities and stick to them rigidly.

A lot of what we have covered may initially have seemed elementary, basic stuff. But I am sure that you have also uncovered some nuggets of wisdom and insight that had not occurred to you before. Remember that it is important to put your new knowledge into action. It is very easy to read something, promise yourself that you'll put it into practice, but then forget all about what you've learned the next time someone makes a request for your time and energy.

Don't give in to old habits, don't follow old patterns, don't say "yes"! Say anything other than "yes". Even if it is really difficult for you, say something that will buy you a little time so you can regroup and come up with a good reason not to help them with their thing. If they're any good at reading signs, they should see your reluctance as a sign. Who knows? Maybe they will offer to ask someone else.

I believe in you and I know that you will take the lessons learned in the book to make a better, more assertive version of you. You are a strong individual who will not stand for that peer pressure. Instead you will maintain your stance and stick to your principles and priorities. There was a reason that you put that list of priorities together and this is it. Remember that it isn't a case of saying "yes", or "no". Instead, it is a case of making the decision that is right for you.

AUTHOR'S NOTE

Thank you so much for taking the time to read my book. I hope you have enjoyed reading this book as much as I've enjoyed writing it. If you enjoyed this book, please consider leaving a review. Your support really means a lot and keeps me going.

If you want more resources like this, follow me on my author profile on Amazon. You will find useful free tools for self development and success that will help you 10X your results.

ABOUT THE AUTHOR

Steven Hopkins is a personal trainer, entrepreneur, life coach, and author on a mission to awaken people to their innate talents and purpose so they can leave their mark in the world.

Steven holds a Master's degree in Behavioral Science and specializes in the areas of success, motivation, self-discipline, communication, NLP techniques, psychology, and human behavior.

When he isn't helping his clients attain their maximum potential, Steven Hopkins enjoys meditating, playing extreme sports, and traveling across the globe. He also loves spending quality time with his lovely wife and his two beautiful children.

Printed in Great Britain
by Amazon